Vigorous Vernacular

Kevin Densley
Vigorous Vernacular

PICARO PRESS

to Steve, Fiona and Kay

Vigorous Vernacular
ISBN 978 1 920957 55 1
Copyright © text Kevin Densley 2008

First published by Picaro Press 2008

This edition published 2018 by
Picaro Press – an imprint of
GINNINDERRA PRESS
PO Box 3461 Port Adelaide 5015 Australia
www.ginninderrapress.com.au

Contents

The Car Chase in Films from Six Different Countries	7
Scarlatti's Pearls	8
Elvis Presley's Late Cheeseburger Period	9
The Ballad of Alexander Pierce	10
said hamlet	11
Young Björn Encounters Sigrid	12
Sylvia Plath in a Bikini	13
Seen from a Window Table in Acland Street, St Kilda	14
Her First and Second Husbands	15
A Short Poem by the Elector of Saxony	16
New Year Kisses	17
Chaconne in F…	18
Brief Sketches of Members of the Kelly Gang	19
Dat Ole Debble Called Redrafting	20
Spleen	21
Stargazy Pie	22
John Keats Was Right	23
Rossini's Truffled Turkey	24
Death 101	25
Ariadne Threadless	26
Adam Lindsay Gordon	27
The Shooting of Fred Lowry	28
Arkwright's Cotton Mill by Moonlight	31
The Dredge Pond, Harrietville, Victoria	32
After Baudelaire	33
The Story of Fisher's Ghost Creek…	34
Pisanello's *The Virgin and Child*…	38
Elsternwick Gothic	39
Concerning the Great Man's Member	40
On First Looking into Homer's Chapbook	41

Feng Shui	42
Swallow This	43
Grandfatherly Metaphysics	44
sexual peccadilloes	45
At Isobel's	46
The Girl in the Giant Wombat Tourist Shop	47
Bread and Circuses	48
Matins	49
What the Phoenicians Took from the Land of Punt	50
Great Literary Fist Fights of the Twentieth Century…	51
The Poem of My Enemy Has Not Been Anthologised	52
Acknowledgements	53

The Car Chase in Films from Six Different Countries

In America, it's Steve McQueen
Ford Mustang crash bang *Bullitt*
streets of San Francisco stuff;
Germany, there's a focus
upon needles on dashboard gauges
rising dangerously into the red;
France, it's a character study:
the wily, corrupt old cop
emotionally torturing
his wet behind the ears sidekick
while letting the villains get away.
In Italy, everything's frantic
– arguing, gesticulating,
crooks and *carabinieri*
equally incompetent.
In India? A series of cuts from the chase
to floridly attired
singing and dancing girls,
jangling bracelets of bells,
while, in Iceland, the car is driven
by an unaccountably nude
unselfconscious blonde au pair,
with her precocious seven-year-old male charge
both passenger and navigator.
Then, in Australia, there is a ute
pursued along a dusty
outback road to vanishing point,
rifle fire, tinnies,
swearing and scattering kangaroos.

Scarlatti's Pearls

little finger-flourishes
on ivory

semiquaver splashes
across black and white keys

crystal rivulets of notes
upon which to run my fingers are these

keyboard sonatas, musical pearls
by Domenico Scarlatti.

He wrote a string of them.

Elvis Presley's Late Cheeseburger Period

The fat man
with the black hair
and the big sideburns
spread his lard across the divan,
ate cheeseburger number five,
shot the television with a magnum handgun
because he hated the six o'clock news,
farted,
took an upper,
got one of his southern airhead aides
to bring the limousine to the front door,
farted again, long and resonantly,
ate a cream puff,
had a heart attack
and died...
Picasso had his blue period,
Van Gogh his early social realist phase,
but the king of rock 'n' roll did not enjoy
a time so elevated
– he simply fell from innocence,
blew up like the Goodyear blimp
and, for a brief time, became his own
middle-aged impersonator.

The Ballad of Alexander Pierce

Back in Van Diemen's Land,
in the good old days,
there was a handsome Irish criminal
named Alexander Pierce.
Apparently, he used to persuade
young convicts to escape with him
solely so he could eat them.

There is no potential for a folk song here.

said hamlet

buggered if I know
              said hamlet
i am mad
      north-by northwest
but today I've
          lost my compass

Young Björn Encounters Sigrid

In every Swedish
adolescent rite-of-passage movie,
there's a blonde busty passionate Amazon,
in her middle twenties,
who startles the virginal teen male lead
by taking off all of her clothes.
She tenderly strips the young man nude
then instructs him, slowly, in the act of love.

Nothing like this ever happened
in my Australian boyhood.

Sylvia Plath in a Bikini

'Sylvia Plath in a Bikini'
– I've had this title in my mind
for a long time now.
I got it from a picture
of (no surprises here!) Sylvia Plath in a bikini,
a picture I saw
whilst flicking through
a book about her life.
What captured my mind at the time, I guess,
was seeing a famous female literary figure
revealed in such a new and surprising way.
One can't imagine a picture
of Charlotte Brontë in a bikini
or George Eliot in a bikini
or, God forbid, Gertrude Stein in one.
What I have to say is this
– there should be more of it.

Seen from a Window Table in Acland Street, St Kilda

Mop-haired palms,
aliens in a wintry park
bereft of its usual suspects
– homeless alcoholics,
students eating lunch.
Luna Park in the rearground,
rickety, resonant
of long-gone picture postcard summers.
Workmen, hippies, businessmen…
a pair of mohawked girls stroll by,
khakied, fit for camouflage
in other, distant jungles.

Her First and Second Husbands

An old school friend of my mother
had a husband and three young kids.
One morning, aged thirty-seven,
he went out to get the milk bottles,
had a heart attack and died.
My mother's friend took twenty years
to marry again.
When she did, it was to a kindly chap
in his early seventies.
After five years of happy marriage,
she woke to find him dead,
more conventionally,
in their marital bed.

Again, the day's milk curdled in the sun.

A Short Poem by the Elector of Saxony

The neurotic man, it has been said,
says, 'I wish I was the King of England.'
The psychotic man, on the other hand,
declares, 'I *am* the King of England.'
The sane man states,
'I am myself, and content to be so.'
What am I, then?
Sometimes I feel
that I'm the King of England;
at other times, I know this can't be true
– how can it be
when I'm really his German half-brother,
the Elector of Saxony?

New Year Kisses

A pair of soft red lips
touches other pairs of soft red lips
in a transient pairs-of-soft-red-lips sea.

Chaconne in F for Recorders, Viola da Gamba and Harpsichord

Such a good title (thank you Henry Purcell)
that I had to
write something
underneath it.

Is this enough?

Brief Sketches of Members of the Kelly Gang

Joe Byrne: balladeer, ladies' man,
spoke Cantonese (he needed
opium from the Chinese),
could hit a penny tossed into the air
with a rifle shot,
Ned's trusted second-in-command.

Steve Hart: ill-tempered,
sometime jockey,
had a mount that could jump the railway gates
at Wangaratta
– his claim to local fame.

Dan Kelly: clever, hawk-eyed,
destined to wear the passed-down clothes
of bigger, older brothers,
useful in a brawl.

Ned Kelly: proud,
crack marksman, fine boxer, trick rider,
addressed women with a parson's manners,
his riastarthae – alexandrite eyes,
born leader, fallen
on the law's wrong side.

Dat Ole Debble Called Redrafting

In the Year of Our Lord 676
Philip of Avalon
entered the Loire Valley
on a pure white Arabian stallion…

In the Year of Grace 676
Philip of Avalon
rode into
the Loire Valley
on a pure white Arabian stallion…

In 676, Philip of Avalon
rode into the Loire Valley
on a pure white Arabian stallion…

Philip of Avalon had a white horse…

Spleen

Spleen,
I want to vent it; got to
get that fist-like
bumpy bluish-red
rubbery organ
and show it to you!
Want you to look long and hard,
as it sits, warm and pulsing, in my hands!
If you're appalled, I don't really care;
in spite of the revulsion
of our sensibilities
and the gut-turning nausea,
the experience will do us
the world of good.
Have a look at my spleen!
I'm busting my guts
to show it to you!

Stargazy Pie

The pilchards in
stargazy pie
look wistfully up
at the evening sky,
open-mouthed and wondering why
they are gazing at the stars.

John Keats Was Right

Keats once said,
'Heard melodies are sweet, but those unheard
Are sweeter.'
– I agree,
so the rest of this poem (except for the next line)
will be out of earshot…

Rossini's Truffled Turkey

Rossini said
there were only three times in his life when he cried:
one, when his first opera failed;
two, when with a boating party,
they lost a truffled turkey over the side
and, three, when he heard Paganini play.

It's not too difficult to guess
over which event he shed the most tears.
He went on to write many successful operas,
must have heard brilliant musicians
on numerous occasions,
but the loss of a truffled turkey!
That would have made the great gourmet
want to write a requiem!

Death 101

Sylvia Plath's
later years
were consumed by study
for this exam,

the very one
where the final result
is never received
by the candidate.

Ariadne Threadless

Trailing a thread behind her,
Ariadne made her way through the maze.
It would be easy to get out
– such was her smug conviction.

But suddenly she turned around
horrified to find the Minotaur
leering, crouched in a corner.
His scissors glinted

in a fleeting shaft of light.

Adam Lindsay Gordon

Adam Lindsay Gordon,
a typical extreme depressive,
lived a hectic, varied life
to help him fill the time.
Slipshod poet,
reckless steeplechase rider,
stuttering South Australian MP…
One dawn, he walked to a Melbourne beach,
put a pistol in his mouth,
then shot a hole through the back of his head
the size of a shilling.
On an early walk,
a man saw his lanky form
branching from the tea trees.

The Shooting of Fred Lowry at Tom Vardy's Limerick Races Hotel, near Goulburn, New South Wales, August 29th, 1863

A cold, still dawn in the bush.
Acting on information,
Senior Sergeant Stephenson
and three other men surrounded the pub.
It was little more than a roadside shack
with a few roughly partitioned rooms.
Fred Lowry and mate Larry Cummins
were holed up there,
having robbed the Mudgee mail coach
the month before.
Stephenson crept along the verandah,
wincing at each creaking board,
then thumped on the bushrangers' door.
'Police! Open up!'
Silence.
He called out again.
'Police! We've got you surrounded!'
Silence still. Broken by a magpie's song.
He shouldered the door, breaking the lock,
then quickly stepped back to one side.
Lowry appeared in the doorway,
a revolver in each hand.

'My name is Lowry!' he declared.
'Come on, I'll fight you fair!'
He fired. Stephenson heard
a bullet singing as it passed his head.
The sergeant's first shot played its own tune,
chiming off the iron door handle.
Lowry fired again. The bullet sparked
off the barrel of Srephenson's gun,
flew inside the sleeve of his cloak
then came out at the elbow
The policeman didn't get a scratch.
He fired a second time,
hitting Lowry in the throat,
throwing him flat on his back.
The sergeant dragged Fred, gurgling blood
and gasping for air, into the clear.
While the other policemen stood guard,
he returned and found Larry Cummins
hiding under the bed. Or, rather, saw Larry's boots sticking out
with Larry still inside them.
A sharp kick. 'Come on, Cummins!'
'It's all right! It's all right!'
came the muffled, frightened reply.
'I'm unarmed! I'm unarmed!'
Larry, head bowed, walked into the yard,
his hands high in the air.
The policemen looked at each other and laughed.

'Oh dear, Larry,' said one, with a grin.
'I believe you've pissed yourself!'
Hours passed. Fred Lowry's life
slowly ebbed away.
He was carried onto a dray
and, with Larry handcuffed at his side,
jolted and bumped towards Goulburn.
Doctor Waugh, at Woodhouseleigh,
a town along the way,
tended to Fred throughout the night
but could do little.
'Internal bleeding,' Waugh explained
to Stephenson, who stifled a yawn.
As day broke, Lowry expired.
All they found in his pockets
was one hundred and sixty pounds in a purse,
part-proceeds from the Mudgee job.
In his post-mortem photo Fred looks a wreck
– a scrawny swaggie in dirty clothes.
Although only twenty-seven,
he'd have passed for a worn-out fifty.

Fred Lowry's career was sorry and brief,
without glamour or reward.
But near the end, he managed to gain
a kind of immortality,
rasping the single most memorable line
in Australian bushranging history:
'Tell 'em I died game.'

Arkwright's Cotton Mill by Moonlight

(a late 18th century painting by Joseph Wright of Derby)

Beehive building
made of stone
caressed
by lunar light;
toilsome, hungry lives
pass within your walls
but still your lambent beauty calls,
sings a lullaby
from the valley of a dark countryside.

The Dredge Pond, Harrietville, Victoria

Very still water,
emerald deep;
bottomless, my mother said.

A dredging operation
in gold rush days
created this water-filled abyss.

I never wanted to swim here.
What if I got tired
and had to touch the bottom?

After Baudelaire

Berenice, I stole
into your darkened bedchamber.
In flaring candlelight we writhed.
I can't recall who did what to whom
in the opium haze
but I remember, in the coal-black sky,
a scimitar moon was hung;
in the morn, a sickly sun;
and the vase on the bedside table was full
of virulent *fleurs du mal*.

The Story of Fisher's Ghost Creek, near Campbelltown, New South Wales

On that morning late in October 1826,
Farley swore he hadn't been drinking the night before.
'No. Not a single drop,' he told the local constable.
'I was driving home about midnight,
coming up to the bridge,
when the horse jibbed, then stopped,
frozen with terror.
Ahead, there was something glowing.
I looked more closely. Couldn't believe my eyes.
It was bloody Fisher,
sitting on a railing on the bridge.'
The policeman stopped stroking his unshaven chin.
He raised his eyebrows.
'Fisher? You mean, Freddy Fisher?'
'Yes. Freddy Fisher.'
'Freddy left the colony a few months back.
Everyone knows that.
You're saying he's returned?'
'Yes, well – sort of,' answered Farley.
'I saw his ghost.'
The policeman sighed, rubbing the sleep from his eyes.
He supposed he had more important work,
but the story was certainly strange.
Copper's instinct told him
he'd better check it out.

'All right, Farley. Let's go have a look.'
In clear morning sunlight, they rode to the bridge.
'Is this the spot?' asked the constable.
'This is it,' answered Farley.
Without dismounting, he placed his hand on the rail.
'Fisher, I mean his ghost,
was sitting just here.'
He patted the weather-worn wood.
'Lift it up,' said the policeman.
'What?'
'Your hand. Lift it up.'
The constable wheeled his horse around.
He examined the faded dark brown stains.
'Wonder where this blood came from?'
'Blood?' asked Farley, taken aback.
'How would I know?'
'It mightn't be anything,' the policeman added, unconvinced.
Vaguely, pieces of a jigsaw puzzle
started to form in his head.
The pair cantered back to town.
'I'll get Threepence to find out what he can,'
the policeman eventually said.
'Anything more you want to add?'
Farley shook his head.

Next day, at the head of a police party,
Threepence the tracker
worked slowly along the banks of the creek.
Finally, he paused.
'I smell white man's fat,' he called out.
A little further,
the men came to a deep pool.
They looked at each other knowingly.
The pool was dragged,
yielding Fisher's months-old remains.
'Worrall,' stated the constable, to no one in particular,
his mental jigsaw puzzle complete.
'I'd better have a word.'
George Worrall lived in the Campbelltown hut
he and Fisher once shared.
When Fisher disappeared, he told everyone
his mate had left the colony
and given him all his worldly goods.
'Restless soul, Fisher,' Worrall observed.
'Left in a hurry… Generous too.'
At the time, no one was greatly surprised
– many freed convicts were wanderers
and did eccentric things.
Years spent in penal servitude,
the general populace rightly believed,
made a man strange.

The constable went to Worrall's hut.
He knocked politely. The door creaked ajar.
A worried bushy face peered out.
The interview didn't last long.
'All right. All right. Enough!
I did it. I killed him,'
Worrall, guilt-stricken, confessed.
He'd heard the story of Fisher's ghost
and felt worse ever since.
'That bastard Fisher,' he lamented,
while being led away.
'He's got me from the grave.'
In due course, Worrall was tried and hanged.
The ghost of Frederick Fisher
wasn't mentioned at the trial,
but in the minds of many present
he was there, a perceptible presence,
pleased to see justice done.

And this is the story of Fisher's Ghost Creek,
perhaps the sole creek in the world
to bear the name of a ghost.
The incorporeal Fisher, though,
was far from being the only phantom
to bring a killer to justice
– they do it all the time.

Pisanello's *The Virgin and Child with the Saints George and Anthony Abbot*

Saint George is an oddity
in his big straw hat
– it looks like a sombrero.
The abbot is scowling at him
through a long grey beard.
Obviously, he does not approve
of the slayer's choice in millinery.
Meanwhile, above them,
encircled by flaming blue and gold,
the Virgin and Child
look dark and Middle Eastern

in a completely different realm.

Elsternwick Gothic

In Elsternwick,
large bats fly overhead
on humid summer evenings,
black Gothic silhouettes
against an indigo sky.
They wing into the distance.
Suddenly, Transylvania
is merely a suburb away.

Concerning the Great Man's Member

Napoleon's dick, some years ago,
was offered for auction by Christie's in Paris.
Nobody wanted it at the time.
Perhaps the reserve was too high.

A US urologist, later on,
purchased the upstart Corsican's cock.
It was one inch long, in a dried-up state,
and had obviously seen better days.

The question is irresistible:
did Napoleon suffer from 'little man complex'
on account of his prick?
Or was he actually hung like a mule?

Probably, boringly, the truth's in between.
Unfortunately, we can't ask Josephine!

On First Looking into Homer's Chapbook

'I have only one question,'
I told my friend,
on first looking into Homer's chapbook.
'What the fuck is a chapbook
and how is it different
from books of other kinds?'

'That's two questions,' my friend replied,
shrugging and walking away.

Feng Shui

Don't put a stove in your bathroom,
a toilet in the kitchen.
Never have your front door
directly off the shower recess.
Forget a bedroom larder…

Swallow This

Fauna and Flora went to sea
in a beautiful pea-green boat,
where the former
ate the latter.

Grandfatherly Metaphysics

'What do you want?' asked my grandfather.
'Nothing,' I replied.
'You'll find it in a bottle
in the shed,'
he rejoined.

sexual peccadilloes

'sexual peccadilloes'
                              sound like randy anteaters

At Isobel's

The sea stretching from your front door
to an Antarctic horizon
is a witch's cauldron,
boiling angry blue.

That shovel-headed brutish dog
which badly mauled your cat
affectionately nuzzles my leg
– I pat it out of fear.

The idiot Narnian goat
grazing in your backyard
displaces me with a psychotic stare
– I don't know where I am.

And you don't seem to have the slightest clue
how much you need to feel threatened.

The Girl in the Giant Wombat Tourist Shop

She was sixteen, enthusiastic,
grateful for the job,
pretty, green-eyed, brown-haired…

And what else for a teenage girl
who left school in Year Ten
in a one-horse town

but work in a two-storey wombat
next to a petrol station
selling souvenirs
to people travelling elsewhere?

Bread and Circuses

Picture a feast
fit for a King
or, at least, the proletariat.
(Pies, sauce and beer will do.)
Imagine a gaggle of brass and a monkey
introducing a juggling clown,
a strongman bearing a giant rock,
a bearded lady,
trapeze artistes
lurexed to within an inch of their lives.
The feasters watch the spectacle,
eating, drinking with lunatic glee,
heading, inevitably,
to this poem's title.

Matins

Blackbirds are eating quinces
that have fallen to the ground.
Shirts on the line,
wrung by the wind,
stay wet with last night's rain.
My girl-cat slouches by.
I smoke a cigarette,
drain my cup of tea, now cold,
and stare into the morning.

What the Phoenicians Took from the Land of Punt

My Year Seven:
a Social Studies test.
Important to memorise this:
what did the Phoenicians
take from the land of Punt?
Answer: wood, incense, ivory,
ebony, silver, gold and apes
– thirty years later, I still remember.

But now I'm more sceptical
about my Social Studies book:
were there only these seven things?
And what did the Phoenicians
do with all those monkeys?

Great Literary Fist Fights of the Twentieth Century: Wallace Stevens vs Ernest Hemingway, Key West, Florida, 1936

Hemingway's sister came back from a party,
told Ernest that Wallace Stevens
had called him something bad.
He-man Ernie bristled, declared
he'd find that Stevens and sort him out.
He got to the party. A scuffle ensued
between Ern and tipsy Wally.
Big Ernie knocked even bigger Wal
a couple of times to the ground.
With the only punch he landed, Wal
broke his hand on Hemmy's jaw.
Now in spite of his reputation, Ern
wasn't much of a fighter.
He liked the low blow, the sneak punch,
picked on those (like Wal)
unschooled in the fistic arts.
Anytime he encountered
a man who could really box,
Ernie dropped like a sack of coal.
In his bout with Wallace Stevens, it's clear
the poet, ethically, won on points.

The Poem of My Enemy Has Not Been Anthologised

(with acknowledgement to Clive James)

The poem of my enemy has not been anthologised
and I am glad.
Although, in my time, she won the university prize
for poetry, it was due
to her politicking, personal charms
and ability to arouse
the flaccid professor-poet
who headed our English department.

A sublimely irritating schmoozer,
she was never short of tutoring work
or obscure, unadvertised scholarships
to research the arcane overseas.
But the poem of my enemy has not been anthologised
– she's been cut off at the knees!

Her work has always been crap
– overworked, mannered, obvious stuff,
devoid of unconscious feeling
– written to give the academic
cognoscenti she flutters about
precisely what she knows they want.
Yes! The poem of my enemy has not been anthologised
and I am deliriously, weepingly glad.

I missed out too.

Acknowledgements

Poems in this collection have been published, sometimes in a slightly different form, in *The Adelaide Review*, *Buzzwords* (UK), *Cadenza* (UK), *Centoria*, *core*, *The Journal* (UK), *LiNQ*, *Mattoid*, *micropress oz*, *modpiece*, *Monkey Kettle* (UK), *Muse*, *New England Review*, *Other Poetry* (UK), *Pendulum*, *Quadrant*, *Redoubt*, *Space*, *Tamba*, *Verandah*, *Vernacular* and *Volition*.

Two poems in this volume have also been anthologised: 'Her First and Second Husbands' in *Now That's What I Call Monkey Kettle* (UK) and 'The Poem of My Enemy Has Not Been Anthologised' in *Miracle and Clockwork: the Best of Other Poetry Series Two* (UK).

www.ingramcontent.com/pod-product-compliance
Lightning Source LLC
Chambersburg PA
CBHW070119110526
44587CB00015BA/2666